Women's Problems in Present Society

Jessica V. Gordon

JESSICA V. GORDON

Copyright © 2017 Jessica V. Gordon

ISBN: 1981700862
ISBN-13: 978-1981700868

DEDICATION

This book is dedicated to every man, woman, or child that cares about women's rights.

Men.

Men.

Men.

Men.

Men.

Men.

Men.

Men.

Men.

13

Men.

Men.

Men.

Men.

Men.

Men.

19

Men.

Men.

Men.

Men.

23

Men.

Men.

25

Men.

Men.

Men.

Men.

29

Men.

Men.

31

Men.

Men.

33

Men.

Men.

Men.

Men.

37

Men.

Men.

Men.

Men.

Men.

42

Men.

Men.

44

Men.

45

Men.

Men.

Men.

Men.

49

Men.

Men.

Men.

Men.

53

Men.

54

Men.

Men.

Men.

Men.

Men.

Men.

Men.

61

Men.

62

Men.

Men.

64

Men.

65

Men.

Men.

Men.

Men.

69

Men.

Men.

Men.

Men.

Men.

74

Men.

75

Men.

76

Men.

Men.

Men.

79

Men.

Men.

Men.

Men.

83

Men.

Men.

Men.

Men.

Men.

Men.

Men.

Men.

Men.

Men.

93

Men.

94

Men.

95

Men.

Men.

Men.

Men.

Men.

Men.

Men.

Men.

Men.

Men.

Men.

Men.

Men.

Men.

Men.

Men.

Men.

Men.

Men.

114

Men.

115

Men.

Men.

Men.

Men.

Men.

Men.

Men.

Men.

123

Men.

Men.

Men.

Men.

Men.

Men.

Men.

Men.

Men.

Men.

133

Men.

Men.

Men.

136

Men.

Men.

Men.

139

Men.

Men.

Men.

Men.

Men.

Men.

145

Men.

Men.

147

Men.

Men.

Men.

Men.

Men.

Men.

Men.

Men.

155

Men.

Men.

Men.

Men.

Men.